ABC Animals
Dot Markers
Activity Book

This Book Belongs To:

Description

AN ANIMALS DOT MARKERS ACTIVITY BOOK FOR KIDS IS A FUN AND INTERACTIVE WAY FOR YOUNG CHILDREN

TO LEARN ABOUT DIFFERENT ANIMALS WHILE ALSO DEVELOPING THEIR FINE MOTOR SKILLS.

THE BOOK CONTAINS PAGES WITH BLACK AND WHITE ANIMAL ILLUSTRATIONS THAT ARE DIVIDED INTO SMALL

SECTIONS OR DOTS. CHILDREN USE DOT MARKERS, WHICH ARE MARKERS WITH ROUNDED TIPS THAT CREATE

CIRCULAR SHAPES WHEN PRESSED ONTO PAPER, TO FILL IN THE DOTS

AND BRING THE ANIMALS TO LIFE WITH VIBRANT COLORS.

THE ANIMAL ILLUSTRATIONS MAY INCLUDE A VARIETY OF CREATURES SUCH AS

FARM ANIMALS, JUNGLE ANIMALS, SEA CREATURES, AND MORE.

EACH PAGE MAY ALSO INCLUDE FUN FACTS ABOUT THE ANIMALS OR SIMPLE ACTIVITIES THAT ENCOURAGE CHILDREN

TO USE THEIR CREATIVITY AND IMAGINATION.

FOR EXAMPLE,

THERE MAY BE A PAGE WITH A JUNGLE SCENE WHERE CHILDREN CAN USE THE DOT MARKERS TO COLOR

IN THE DIFFERENT ANIMALS AND THEN USE STICKERS OR OTHER MATERIALS TO CREATE A HABITAT FOR THEM.

OVERALL, AN ANIMALS DOT MARKERS ACTIVITY BOOK IS A FUN AND EDUCATIONAL TOOL THAT CAN HELP CHILDREN

LEARN ABOUT DIFFERENT ANIMALS WHILE ALSO IMPROVING THEIR

HAND-EYE COORDINATION, CONCENTRATION, AND CREATIVITY.

Aa   is for   Aligator
Bb   is for   Bear
Cc   is for   Cat
Dd   is for   Dog
Ee   is for   Elephant
Ff   is for   Fox
Gg   is for   Giraffe
Hh   is for   Horse
Ii   is for   Iguana
Jj   is for   Jelly Fish
Kk   is for   Kangaroo
Ll   is for   Lion
Mm   is for   Mouse

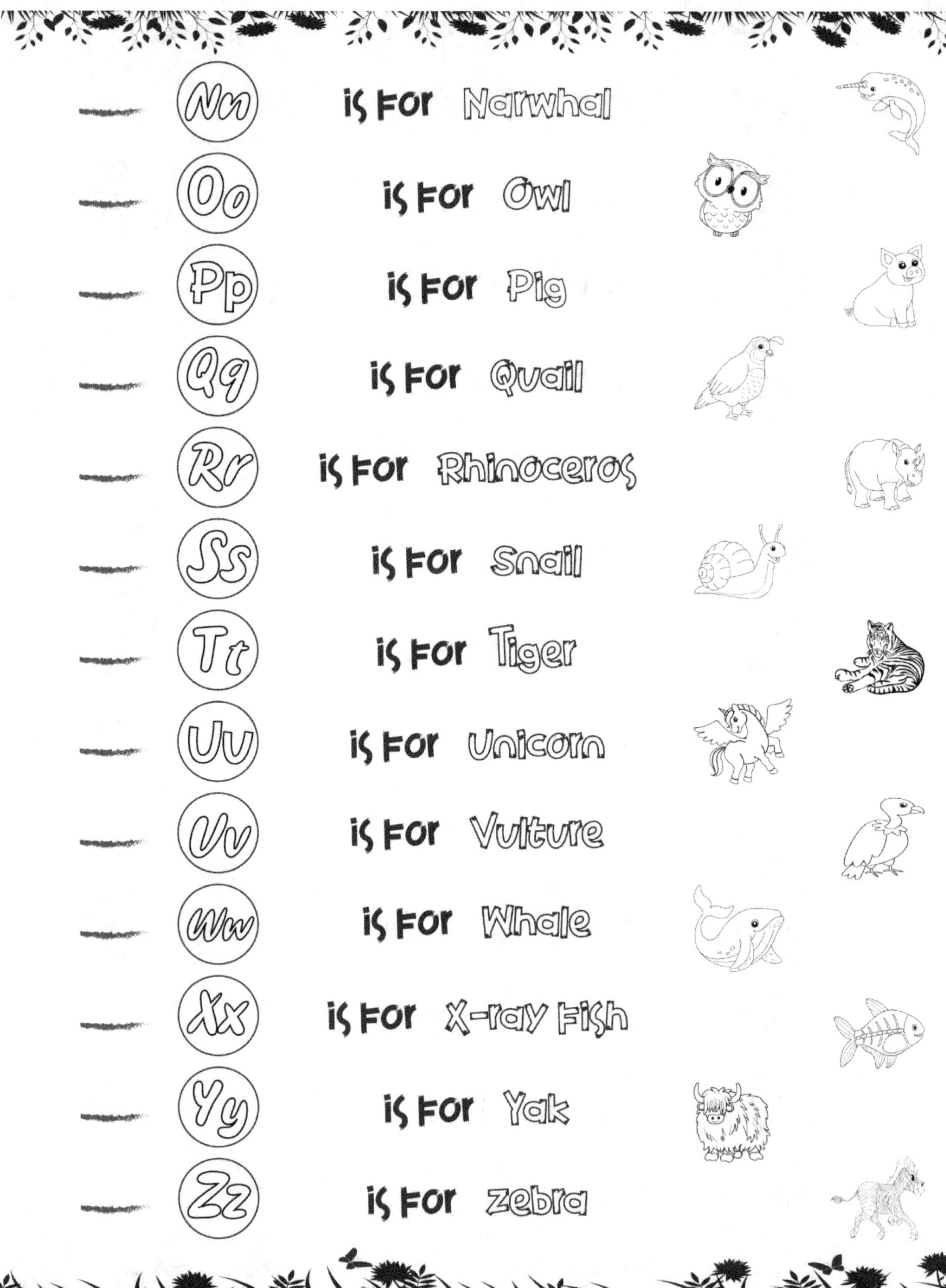

_____ (Nn) is for Narwhal
_____ (Oo) is for Owl
_____ (Pp) is for Pig
_____ (Qq) is for Quail
_____ (Rr) is for Rhinoceros
_____ (Ss) is for Snail
_____ (Tt) is for Tiger
_____ (Uu) is for Unicorn
_____ (Vv) is for Vulture
_____ (Ww) is for Whale
_____ (Xx) is for X-ray Fish
_____ (Yy) is for Yak
_____ (Zz) is for Zebra

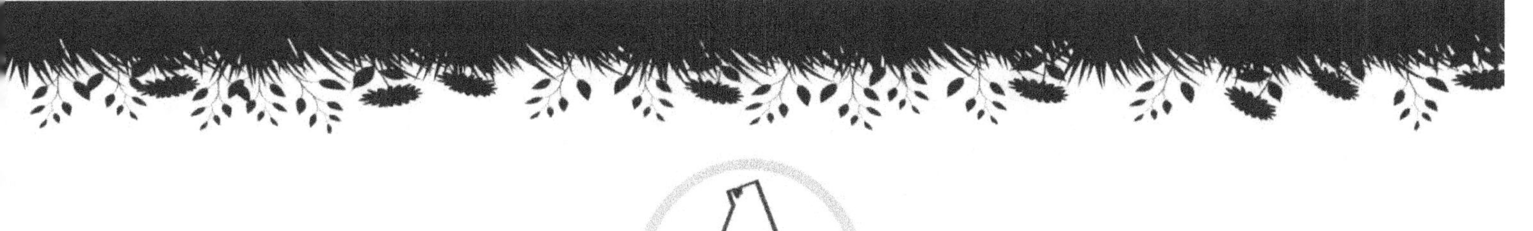

Aligator

B

Bear

C
Cat

D
Dog

E

Elephant

F f

G g

H h

I i

J j

F
Fox

G
Giraffe

H
Horse

I

Iguana

J
Jelly Fish

Kk
Ll
Mm
Nn
Oo

K
Kangaroo

L
Lion

M
Mouse

N
Narwhal

O
Owl

Pp

Qq

Rr

Ss

Tt

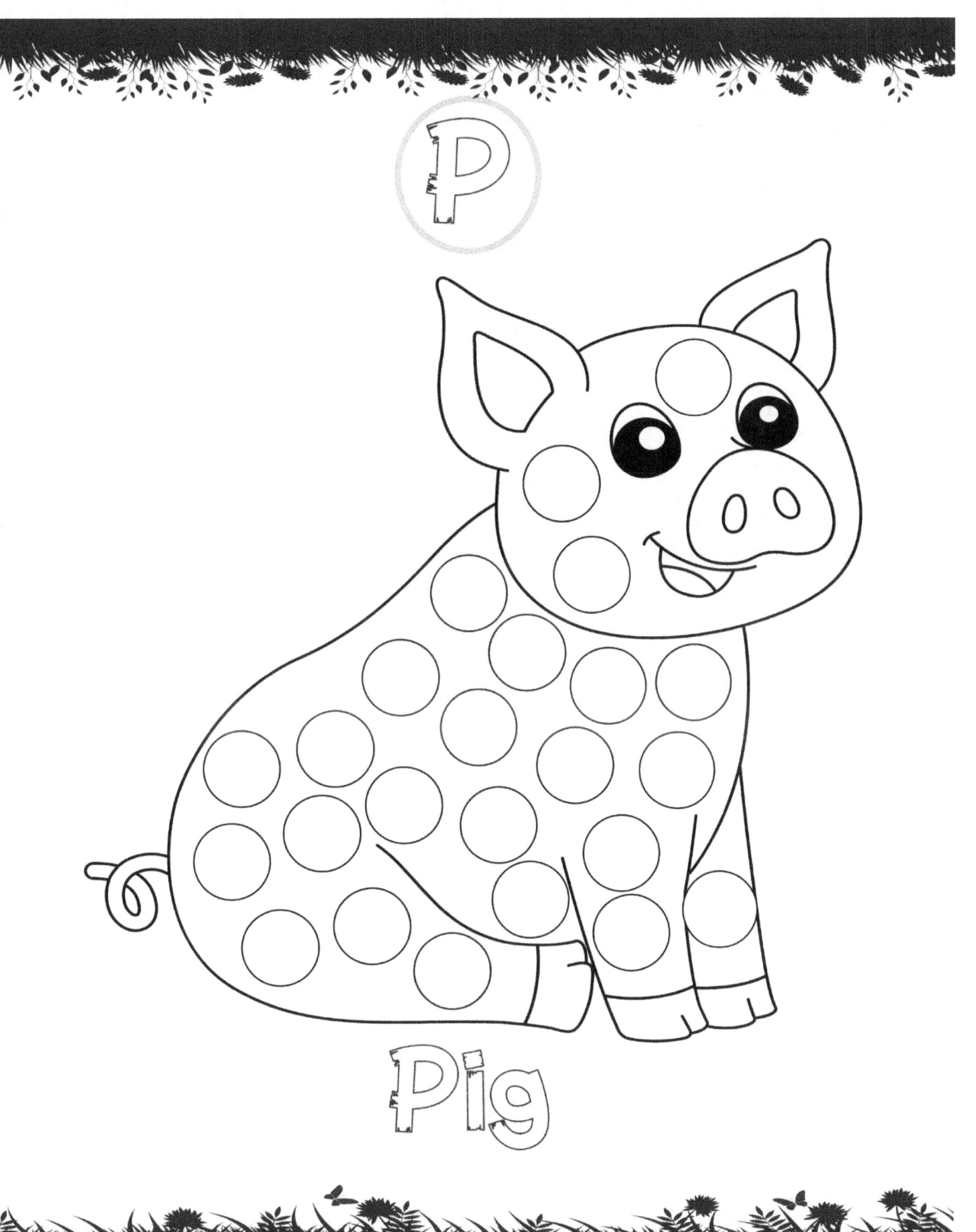

P
Pig

Q
Quail

Rhinoceros

S
Snail

T
Tiger

Uu Vv

Ww Xx

Yy Zz

U
Unicorn

Vulture

W
Whale

X-ray Fish

Y
Yak

Z
zebra

<u>Giving Thanks</u>

"Dear parents,

I wanted to take a moment to express my heartfelt thanks for choosing my book,

"ABC Dot Markers,"

to help your children learn the alphabet.

It brings me great joy to know that your little ones are enjoying the book

and benefiting from its content.

As a children's author, there's nothing more rewarding than seeing kids engage with

and enjoy the books that I create. Your support and encouragement mean the world to me,

and I'm grateful for the opportunity to be a part of your child's learning journey.

I hope that "ABC Dot Markers" has been a valuable resource for you and your family.

If there's anything else I can do to support your child's learning and development,

please don't hesitate to reach out.

Once again, thank you so much for your support and

for choosing my book to help your children learn and grow.

Best regards,

By: Richard Bohan